WAITING FOR MORNING

SEEKING GOD IN OUR SUFFERING

JAMES R. KOK

CRC Publications
Grand Rapids, Michigan

Waiting for Morning: Seeking God in Our Suffering, © 1997 by CRC Publications, 2850 Kalamazoo Ave. SE, Grand Rapids, MI 49560.

Library of Congress Cataloging-in-Publication Data

Kok, James R., 1935-
    Waiting for morning: seeking God in our suffering/James R. Kok.
      p. cm.
    ISBN 1-56212-268-1
    1. Suffering—Religious aspects—Christianity. 2. Consolation.
    I. Title.
    BT732.7.K65 1997
    248.8'6—dc21   97-35582
                                                  CIP

10 9 8 7 6 5 4 3 2 1

To my wife, Linda, an inspiration to all of us
in and through very trying circumstances.
Her credible testimony to the healing power
of prayer, cheerful hopefulness,
steady strength, calm resilience,
and simple trust in God modeled
for everybody how to face adversity.

CONTENTS

PREFACE

Why? What is the purpose of it? Why me? Am I the only one? Does it really make me closer to God? Did you do it, God? Or are you as helpless in the face of it as I? What did I do to deserve this? Is this punishment?

God's people have always asked questions in the face of suffering—both their own suffering and the suffering of others they love. Jim Kok answers them. Not with explanations. Not with reasoned theological arguments. He answers them as a pastor. He knows that the right response to "Why me?" is often "Lo, I will be with you, even to the end of the world."

Jim Kok's replies—they are more replies than answers—belong to the wisdom tradition. For example, he understands the value of denial, that emotional anesthetic that cushions us from the full impact of our pain. There are times when facing reality is too much; it would destroy us. So God gives us the grace of partial understanding and of partial answers, necessary for temporary survival.

The wisdom in this book knows the peculiarities of pain. In their suffering some people turn from their godlessness to their Savior. For some suffering ripens into service. Some take the way of bitterness. Some know all the answers to suffering and never benefit from it.

Jim Kok knows that no answer can finally settle the voice of the skeptic within us. In the sidebars of many pages the inner voice that questions God, the voice that wrestles God to the ground, echoes the voice of faith: "Is it really true?" "Are you really there, God?" "Do you really care?"

This is not a book of easy answers. Kok struggles in pain but also in faith and comes finally to embrace God. Rather, he comes finally to find God embracing him.

MELVIN D. HUGEN
Professor of Pastoral Care
Calvin Theological Seminary

Sorrow is better
than laughter,
because a sad face is good
for the heart.

ECCLESIASTES 7:3

1
MINING POSITIVES FROM NEGATIVES

*What should be the final
outcome of our suffering?*

I stood on the first tee at a fancy country club. I was coerced into entering this tournament, so I felt self-conscious and nervous as a dozen excellent golfers waited for me to hit my initial drive. My mediocrity never loomed larger. Finally I swung. True to my self-belittling prophecies the little ball soared long and far, then sliced into the wretched knee-high weeds.

I waded into the weeds with little hope of locating the errant projectile. And I didn't. But my futile search turned up five lost balls others had lost. Still embarrassed about my bad shot, I perked up at my good fortune. Momentarily I even considered staying in the weeds, leaving the game, and collecting golf balls instead. But, of course, I didn't. Still sick about my horrible shot, slightly lifted by the half-dozen like-new golf balls in my bag, I rejoined the others and hacked on. Gradually the errant slice slid from memory. But the satisfaction of my unexpected find lingered a little longer.

My impaired golf shot does not qualify as suffering. But look at the parallels. Good discoveries accompany life's unwanted episodes—even the meanest tornado—if we have the will to find them. Of course, finding something valuable never erases the agony of the original devastation. But good is there somewhere if we are willing to pick it up.

WHAT STORIES DO YOU HAVE OF SIMILAR EVENTS IN YOUR LIFE—PAINFUL SITUATIONS THAT LED TO SOMETHING GOOD? GO AHEAD AND TELL SOME.

STUCK IN THE WEEDS

The rewards we scavenge after a storm seldom compensate for our original loss—I'd quickly trade in the five golf balls I found for a straight drive to the middle of the fairway. Nor is it sensible to say that tragedy happens *in order that* we can gain certain treasures.

Disabled by a major stroke, my friend Ted was sidelined for months from his active life as an executive. Today, several years later, he has mastered the computer and created a service business more lucrative and satisfying than his original work. Thoughtful Christians will not think that God sent the stroke to open up this new opportunity. Circumstances triggered Ted's stroke. Yet God helped him start over.

The temptation to stay in the weeds and abandon the game arises within all of us. Some fringe benefits from suffering can become addictive. When we seize them, we don't easily release them.

HAVE YOU EVER WANTED TO "STAY IN THE WEEDS"? WHEN? WHY?

Lyn's son was kidnaped and murdered a decade and a half ago. At that time, life stopped for Lyn as well. Attention, well-deserved compassion, deeply needed sympathy, and publicity fed Lyn's ravaged soul beyond anything she had ever known. For fifteen years now, she's been in the weeds, living on the crumbs of compassion that others originally provided generously but now dole out reluctantly—just enough pity, when supplemented by her own, to keep Lyn from getting up and rejoining the living. We sometimes grasp the slim benefits of tragedy so tightly that we forfeit the solid satisfactions of our lives.

WORKING TOGETHER FOR GOOD

When the apostle Paul writes that "in all things God works for the good of those who love him . . ." (Rom. 8:28), he doesn't mean that this will happen immediately or automatically. Nor does he mean that we will always see how this happens or that the new good will always surpass what we had before. And he doesn't promise that our new state will erase all our pain. I think he means that God's trusting pilgrims will eventually find riches in every smashing experience—if we look, if we decide, if we are open.

HAVE YOU HEARD WELL-MEANING PEOPLE QUOTE THESE WORDS IN A WAY THAT MAKES YOU WANT TO STRANGLE THEM DESPITE THEIR GOOD INTENT?

A very expensive Aeolian Skinner pipe organ stands in place in the Arboretum Hall of the Crystal Cathedral. Our organist and director of music, Fred Swann, calls it "a Stradivarius, a jewel." We acquired the seasoned, old instrument at a bargain-basement price after the 1994 Northridge earthquake. The church building of the congregation we purchased it from had been condemned because of damage from the quake. But the organ stood unscathed. A sad time for that congregation turned into a benefit for us.

When we dedicated the organ in our Arboretum, Dr. Swann invited the members of the original church to a concert in their honor. The response was strong. Nearly the whole congregation showed up and celebrated the organ's rebirth with cheers, applause, and tears. It was a day of joy and thanksgiving to God. Their broken building could not be repaired. The revered organ needed adoption. This beautiful new location offered a bright new life for the instrument. So we all celebrated. Even though we all preferred things the way they used to be, going back was not possible. So we had to leave the past behind and embrace the new situation.

As enthusiastic members of both churches, we attribute to God this happy solution: life after death on a minor scale.

GO BACK TO PAUL'S WORDS IN ROMANS 8:28. HOW DO THEY APPLY ON THE MAJOR SCALE?

13

DON'T RENAME TO AVOID RECALL

Something else also happens regularly when we find ourselves in bad circumstances. About once a week, in the wee hours of the morning, I wake up with a small headache. After falling back asleep I awaken at dawn with a roaring pain that dominates my skull and fully clouds the next eight hours of my life, no matter what I swallow. Naturally I mention my malaise to those close to me, my father among them. He shows appropriate concern and then invariably claims, "I have never had a headache."

For several years this little drama has repeated itself now and then. But recently I countered his claim. I recalled his serious sinus discomfort during his younger years:

"Your sinus trouble caused you headaches, didn't it?"

"That was a sinus problem."

"Oh, I see, if you name it something different it isn't a headache. That's how they got rid of cockroaches in Florida. They just changed their name to 'banana bugs.'"

In a much more perilous setting, the prophet Jeremiah speaks to this unholy tendency: "They dress the wound of my people as though it were not serious. 'Peace, peace,' they say, when there is no peace" (Jer. 6:14).

The *Living Bible* paraphrases this as: "You can't heal a wound by saying it's not there."

WHAT MAKES US WANT TO DENY OUR PAIN? CAN YOU GIVE AN EXAMPLE FROM YOUR OWN EXPERIENCE?

But that is how some folks handle suffering. They deny it. Or they call it by another name. Some even call what they suffer a "blessing."

MOVING THROUGH OUR PAIN

As with my dad's headaches, though, the pain is usually still there. Putting a positive spin on it can help a little. Living in some denial is not always a bad idea. But most often we're not able to derive a bona fide blessing from an ill wind until after a lot of time has passed. The perspective distance brings grinds down the rough edges slowly.

Maximum spiritual gains trickle from frank and earnest dismay, from wrestling with God with all our might, from feeling our pain without denial. Empty-handed anguish is the starting block of our rebirth. Resurrection follows death. Prayer, lament, study, caring people, and conversation help our suffering to congeal into strong spiritual muscle. The positives we mine from our negatives are well-earned. The objective we aim for after our calamities have their way is to find those good nuggets and let them enrich our lives. The goal toward which we stretch is new life after death.

THIS PARAGRAPH SURVEYS AT WARP SPEED THE PROCESS BY WHICH WE CAN GENUINELY MINE THE GOOD FROM OUR BAD EXPERIENCES. PICK OUT AND DESCRIBE THE STEPS IT SUGGESTS. ARE THERE OTHER STEPS YOU CAN THINK OF?

We know that the whole creation has been groaning as in the pains of childbirth right up to the present time. . . . We ourselves, who have the firstfruits of the Spirit, groan inwardly as we wait eagerly for . . . the redemption of our bodies.

ROMANS 8:22-23

2

SUFFERING IS EVERYWHERE

Is suffering common or rare,
widespread or just here and there?

To live means to suffer. We suffer whenever we face, walk through, or are trapped by circumstances that we strongly detest or badly want to escape. We suffer when we're denied, lose, or are deprived of significant, irreplaceable hopes or relationships. Pain—physical, social, emotional, mental, or spiritual—that does not go away is another way that suffering grips God's children. Our worst suffering includes the three dimensions of pain: physical pain, psychological/spiritual anguish, and social degradation.

The suffering of Jesus clearly contains all of these. He was "despised and rejected" (Isa. 53:3). The leaders and masses alike set aside and discounted his goodness. His friends betrayed him. Though he was innocent, he was hammered, whipped, and killed. Few among us suffer all that Jesus did: physical pain and impairment, spiritual

DOES YOUR OWN LIFE, OR THE LIFE OF SOMEONE CLOSE TO YOU, VERIFY THAT OUR WORST SUFFERING INCLUDES ALL THREE OF THESE DIMENSIONS OF SUFFERING?

doubts, feelings of abandonment, psychological torment, and loss of status in the community.

DIFFERING THRESHOLDS OF SUFFERING

We all suffer. But we do not all receive the same amount of this unwanted stuff. Life is certainly not fair in the way it hands out pain, denial, disappointment, and deprivation. For no apparent reason, some folks get way more than their share. Others get off easy.

RELATE SOME EXAMPLES OF THIS PHENOMENON FROM YOUR OWN EXPERIENCE.

The way we experience similar kinds of suffering also varies from person to person. Just after Thanksgiving, I buried my family's twelve-year-old black Lab under the nectarine tree in the backyard. It was a sad day. Still is. But it's a small thing in the annals of suffering—for me, at least. Another person might find such a loss gigantic and recovery from it difficult. A minor heartbreak for one may be a world-class tragedy for another.

Recently I was asked to return a call to a distraught man in a distant state. His story surprised me. At age fifty he was in deep pain over the death of his grandmother. Empathy eluded me at first. I assumed that, by his age, he should be able to handle such a loss easily. He should have long anticipated the demise of this aged family member and been well on his way through the grieving process when she died. I assumed wrongly.

CONSPICUOUS AND HIDDEN SUFFERING

If we were to classify hurts, nothing measures up to the loss of a child—by death, or by some other way. There are other excruciating pains, but few come close to the wrongness of this one. I count as friends several parents who have lost children. Describing their pain is not possible, even for them.

Lorie's two toddlers were cold-bloodedly murdered by their father, her estranged husband. Today he awaits trial in Orange County Jail. She drags on with life, numb with grief too deep even for tears. Words fail too. Her loss defies expression. Life hands out nothing worse.

There are conspicuous sufferers like Lorie. Their plights are obvious and known. There are also hidden sufferers. Hidden sufferers may outnumber all others and they receive a lot less support. Their suffering is acute but more subtle. It's immense but invisible to others.

DO YOU AGREE THAT HIDDEN SUFFERERS OUTNUMBER ALL OTHERS? EXPLAIN.

Eloise is a fine-looking, articulate woman in her early sixties. The business she's established by herself thrives, and she dresses smartly, illustrating her prosperity. But one day I happened to scratch through her glossy exterior by inquiring about her lifelong singleness. Self-assurance and success melted away as her secret pain spilled out. Her hopes and dreams of a secure marriage unraveled in secret pain as the number of her years added up.

Hidden sufferers often experience the hurt of a dream or a hope that has died. They reach a point of no return and know, or strongly fear, that their longed-for aspiration will never be realized or fulfilled. They journey on, privately holding in their hearts the death of their dream.

I met Jack and Juanita at his bedside at St. Jude's hospital. Jack was fighting for life with a severe illness. In the process of getting to know Juanita, I inquired if their thirty-six-year marriage included children. The question brought an immediate flow of tears to her eyes. I had stumbled into her long-held, secret grief, a pain she carried privately all the years of their life together. Her husband was dying, but in the vault of her heart lurked another long-term personal sorrow.

IS IT OK FOR SUFFERING TO REMAIN HIDDEN? HOW SHOULD WE COME TO TERMS WITH HIDDEN SUFFERING IN OURSELVES AND IN OTHERS?

A CATALOG OF CARES

Afflictions, diseases, illnesses, and severe disabilities count among the most disheartening and agonizing conditions. They show up everywhere, in an endless number of forms ranging from Alzheimer's to birth defects, from cancer to chronic pain, from depression to multiple sclerosis. Add addiction, rage, lawlessness, irresponsibility, perversity, and lovelessness, and another huge category of suffering springs to mind.

21

DOES A PERSON'S
RESPONSIBILITY FOR
HIS OR HER PAINFUL
CONDITION
INCREASE OR
DECREASE THE LEVEL
OF SUFFERING? GIVE
SOME EXAMPLES.
HOW SHOULD WE
RESPOND IN
SITUATIONS WHERE
SUFFERING IS AT
LEAST PARTIALLY SELF-
INFLICTED?

HOW CAN WE FACE
DEATH WITH
COURAGE—THE
DEATH OF OUR
LOVED ONES, AS
WELL AS OUR OWN?

Life is full of pain. Not the least of it may be the social, psychological, and physical angst of just being an acne-plagued teenager who feels ugly and unlovable.

There are far more calamities and tragedies than we can list here. But one more needs mentioning. In a very real way all humankind suffers together in this one common affliction—always has, always will. It's the inescapable realization that we and our loved ones are scheduled, sooner or later, to die. Death, far more than we realize, controls, motivates, inhibits, and accelerates what we do and how we think.

Our terminal condition hangs over our heads and affects us with little hope for a solution, except one. The one hope is a faith hope. That answer, the Easter answer, embraced by millions of people, can sneak a smile on a tear-stained heart and break through hardened dead-end worries. But it is a joy reserved for those who acknowledge their distress over having to part with loved ones and who boldly acknowledge they will someday die themselves.

SUFFERING'S EFFECTS

WHAT ACCOUNTS
FOR THIS
UNEXPECTED RETURN
TO HAPPINESS AFTER
PERIODS OF
SUFFERING? CAN
YOU GIVE EXAMPLES?

This I have discovered: suffering and unhappiness are not synonyms. They are not even necessarily connected. Suffering certainly attacks well-being. But all who suffer intensely are not destined to be stuck in unhappiness. We can find people of great hope and steady joy among the ranks of the badly devastated. Likewise, those with light loads are not always the happiest folks around. We all know miserable people whose circumstances look pleasant and enviable to us but who still dwell in gloom and pessimism. Overall, most of us who have gone through truly hard times and extreme suffering move along to be reasonably happy as years go by. Few people allow their suffering to define them forever as miserable people. Most recover.

When we look closely at those around us, another surprising picture emerges. The least attractive, least interesting, and least credible people turn out to be those who have suffered little. Those who are deep, believable, and wise have been through a lot. So while we do not want suffering, we can salvage it, recycle it, and turn it into the very best stuff. In fact, we cannot acquire the very best stuff of life in any other way.

Suffering appears to be a necessary evil, a bad thing that possesses ingredients that can bring good. In our everyday lives we are surrounded by an elite corps of fighters. These troops know secrets at a level that most of us cannot reach. These soldiers have been drafted through the selective service of suffering. They know God better. They perceive what is truly important. They understand life in ways that only their fellow wounded ones know. These are the wise. They are the wounded. The wise have usually been wounded. Unfortunately, not all who are wounded grow wise.

Life is difficult. The challenges and threats to our well-being—real or imagined—are infinite in number and kind. I believe that's why our Creator God revealed himself to us. God's heart broke over our lostness. God worked a plan to help us be people of hope in a hazardous world. God comes and brings new promise to weak people who inevitably slam into walls and get knocked down by loaded freight trains. Getting up again works best when we reach our hands up to our loving Lord.

DESCRIBE THIS "VERY BEST STUFF" THAT WE CAN GAIN FROM OUR SUFFERING.

THIS CLAIM NEEDS SOME DEMONSTRATION. CAN YOU PROVIDE SOME EXAMPLES?

SUFFERING IS EVERYWHERE. IS THERE COMFORT IN THE FACT THAT GOD IS EVERYWHERE AS WELL? EXPLAIN.

He longed to fill his stomach with the pods that the pigs were eating, but no one gave him anything. When he came to his senses, he said . . . "I will set out and go back to my father."

LUKE 15:16-18

3

SPIRITUAL GROWTH AND HUMAN SUFFERING

Do the afflictions so common to our lives really generate and facilitate greater reliance on, understanding of, and devotion to God?

An elder told me about a phone call she made in connection with her office. The woman she spoke to had deflected the purpose of the call by asking, "Did you know my husband was killed in November?" She then told the story of how the young high school coach had been shot as he knelt alongside his BMW to change a flat tire. As the conversation progressed, the elder delicately inquired whether the young woman had religious faith. She replied, "I was active when I was young. Now that is all I have."

Dormant seeds, sown in childhood, apparently destined to lie useless in the desert of her life, were now germinating, irrigated by this tragedy. New life stirred in her like chicks breaking out of their shells. Pain and struggle lay ahead, but a positive metamorphosis also appeared on her horizon. Conventional wisdom insists that hard times and suffering cause people to grow spiritually.

TEST THIS ASSERTION A BIT. DOES YOUR EXPERIENCE CONFIRM THAT SUFFERING CAN BRING SPIRITUAL GROWTH?

Very little spiritual growth or any other kind of growth germinates in adults who do not experience pain, difficulty, or perplexity. Smooth sailing offers the least fertile environment for our deepening as human beings or in our relationship with the Lord. God's loving presence surrounds us all the time. But we are more likely to respond positively and reach out fervently when the going gets rough.

TURNING SINNERS INTO SAINTS

A few days ago a dapper young man came to see me. He wanted to confess to a crime. His good life was coming apart as a consequence of a stupid decision that had now been exposed. Jail time loomed as a real possibility. We talked of God and forgiveness. His soul and his eyes spilled over with remorse, repentance, and determination to change.

Spiritual growth appears to be underway in this man's life. That's why I couldn't help secretly rejoicing over the quagmire in which he had trapped himself. I was thinking, "If he hadn't screwed up his life so stupidly, this good stuff might never have gotten started."

WHY IS THAT SO? WHY DOES IT TAKE SUFFERING TO MOVE OUR SOULS TOWARDS GOD?

This scenario of sad times turning folks into saints is pleasingly common. Stories abound of flattened people getting up and becoming more than they ever were in relation to God. Mostly it's when life harshly cracks through our defensive armor that something beneficial happens to our souls. Sad to say, it often takes disruption to get things going in the right direction. Robert Hestene says that three basic commodities of life—wealth, sleep, and health—will not be appreciated until they are interrupted. We can expand his observation to include much more.

Suffering turns many a godless man or woman to God. Far more than they ever notice or realize, tragedy slips godly folks forward and upward into new heights of spirituality. Their improved lives make sense out of the strange words Paul speaks in Romans 5: 3, "we rejoice in our sufferings."

We do, but rarely while they are happening. Paul speaks philosophically. He knows this important reality personally. But he is not calling us to laugh when our hearts are breaking.

REALIZING OUR NEED

I carry fresh in my memory the story of a young college student raped at gunpoint in her inner-city apartment. Smashed psychologically, battered physically, her faith in God was as good as dead. She had moved boldly to what was known as a dangerous neighborhood because she so strongly trusted the Lord to care for her and protect her. Fearlessly she countered the advice of family and friends, calling it faithless. Now her spiritual backbone lay shattered—but not quite totalled. The attack had disillusioned her. She needed to be disillusioned. Now under construction in her is faith that realistically and appropriately combines good sense with a faithful Lord, ever present and always caring. Her spiritual growth is inching forward.

One reason suffering wields such power is that it pummels us into empty-handedness, into a spiritual resourcelessness that only God can fill. That is where the young murdered coach's wife found herself—helpless, out-of-control, powerless. Suffering easily destroys the illusions we have that we are in control of our lives. It forces us to look for and embrace a support system that will not fail, a presence that will never leave us. Suffering can knock us to our knees and impel us to look upward. Suffering can shatter our foolish self-confidence, which often exceeds appropriate boundaries of humility. Then, finally, the promise of God to never leave us or forsake us begins to take hold and salve our wounded souls. Then Jesus' invitation, "Come to me, all you who are weary and burdened" (Matt. 11:28), takes on its full meaning.

SHOULD OUR SPIRITUAL GROWTH REQUIRE SUCH A DEVASTATING EXPERIENCE? IS IT EVER WORTH SUCH COST? AREN'T THERE BETTER WAYS TO GROW SPIRITUALLY?

Jesus recommended to a rich young man that he sell all he had and give the proceeds to the poor. Jesus diagnosed his spiritual peril. The young man was too well protected and insulated by his material possessions. Having so much, he might not experience enough discomfort to teach him his need for God. Poverty is not a guaranteed mover, but like other kinds of suffering, it too has the potential to stir our souls toward God. Affluence, on the other hand, like perfect health, easily moves us into a dangerous smugness. We harbor the illusion that we're firmly in control. Too much or too little of anything, even our own sense of well-being, holds real spiritual hazards.

WHAT'S WRONG WITH HARBORING THE NOTION THAT WE'RE IN CONTROL OF OUR LIVES? WHAT DOES THE BIBLE TEACH?

IN HINDSIGHT . . .

People who find a new or special kinship with God as a consequence of their suffering frequently speak retrospectively. It stands to reason. When you've just been hit by a freight train, all that matters is that you manage to get another gulp of air. When we're first smashed to smithereens by tragedy, we may be able to manage nothing more than gasping a brief prayer. Spiritual growth may be in the long-range forecast, but for the moment, survival is all we can think about. Rejoicing over our suffering—Paul's words—is something we cannot claim credibly until most of the initial bleeding of our hearts has stopped.

Only later a testimony may emerge about feeling God's presence, sensing the Lord's steadying hand, or surviving only by God's grace. After a long time, maybe years, we might salvage more evidence of spiritual enhancement from the wreckage.

IS SUCH A TESTIMONY ONLY A BACKWARD PROJECTION OF SOMETHING THAT DIDN'T REALLY EXIST WHEN WE WERE GOING THROUGH OUR CRISIS?

In my own life, I discovered only several decades later that my mother's youthful death enhanced the independence and self-reliance that I needed to grow up. Besides that, my own confused wandering made me pay attention to the perplexities and pain of loss and grief.

STILL WATERS RUN DEEP

Spiritual growth is a mysterious and undefinable process. Not all who talk articulately of what they have discovered spiritually deserve the main spotlight. The most credible are rarely glib about broadcasting their gains. Those who are truly deepened usually reflect it quietly. They move through subtle changes. Surefootedness slows to uncertainty. Perky independence changes to childlikeness. Superficiality digs down to calm depth. Those who were uncaring become compassionate. Those who were object-oriented now value the relational. To them, people have become more important than things. We see the essence of much of their spiritual growth in their fresh appreciation that the frantic pace and feverish grasping of everyday life is foolish and futile.

A long, tough fight with illness changed Stan. His "make every minute count" attitude had driven him into a high level of engineering excellence. But life now looked different. Previously he had chided his young adult son for wasting time watching televised sports. Now he invited him to join him in enjoying NCAA basketball play-offs. Before his diagnosis, there never seemed to be space for going to church. Now he never missed a Sunday. Everything looked different as uncertainty defined his life span. Clobbered by leukemia, Stan finally woke up.

WHAT ARE *YOUR* PRIORITIES IN LIFE? WHAT *SHOULD* THEY BE? WHAT WILL IT TAKE FOR YOU TO SLOW DOWN ENOUGH TO DO A CAREFUL SPIRITUAL INVENTORY?

FINDING GOD'S PROMISE

Growth nearly always includes new insight that what really matters is the security and goodness of God's healing promises. When the surgery of sorrow opens our hearts, we find, maybe for the first time in our lives, what "the peace that passes understanding" really feels like. And yet the vise of pain may never totally loosen. When we are really hurt, we seldom leave it all behind once and for all. We live on, seasoned by an unending ache in a corner of our hearts.

One young couple struggled long and hard with the challenge of infertility, then conceived a child. Joy like a spring rain turned their wasteland into a flower garden. Belief tiptoed back. "God lives and cares!" their hearts cried. Sometime later I asked, "How has your life changed through all this?"

WHAT TOOLS HAS GOD USED TO MOVE YOU ALONG IN YOUR SPIRITUAL LIFE?

Their answer surprised me. "We don't dance anymore," they replied. They explained that their life was deeper, more serious after all they'd gone through. Dancing was fine. They didn't expect to abandon it forever. But it represented carefree times and youthful lightheartedness. God used the pain and heartache of their barren years to shave away the glossy surface of their characters, turning them to softheartedness and seriousness.

WHEN SUFFERING RIPENS INTO SERVING

People who speak of growing spiritually increase in credibility when their inner lives spill over into altered daily living. It is one thing to talk, feel, and even look changed. We take another giant step when bad stuff generates positive good works, when the harsh world is made better by the benevolent and revolutionary actions of recovering victims.

Two women who have become close friends exemplify how we can turn horrific pain into visible, uplifting service. Sharon and Shirley each have lost a teenaged son to suicide. Two healthy boys impulsively ended their lives and shattered their parents' dreams. One son was disappointed in sports. The other was thwarted in romance. In the years that followed their horrific losses, these two moms have become involved in church activities at new levels. Both serve as crisis telephone counselors and invest long hours in training new volunteers. Together they have studied and trained to become resource people in understanding and preventing suicide. They willingly travel wherever they're invited to speak and teach, even though the subject never loses its capacity to plunge them once again into their pain.

Sharon and Shirley don't fluently articulate the spiritual growth they received from their awful tragedies. Their consistent Christian service speaks for them. An award they recently received for outstanding ministry heralds boldly their deep commitment and faithful involvement in a vital campaign to save precious lives. Their new lives emerged from the swamp of sadness and heartache.

SUFFERING IS A SWINGING DOOR

"How can a good God allow a tragedy like that?" she bitterly protested. It was more of a complaint than a question. I treated it that way and didn't attempt an answer. Her challenge cries out like a disruptive heckler in a political rally who gets under the speaker's skin by shouting half-truths. I'll wager that millions have exited their faith through this door of blaming God for failing them. For shallow people, these thoughts offer a convenient rationalization for slamming shut the church door and turning their back on whatever walk they had with God.

Usually a seriously flawed faith laid the groundwork for this kind of disillusionment. With so many others, these people held the false notion that God is a gatekeeper who willingly allows catastrophes to slip through. They're wrong. Except for natural disasters, catastrophes are the by-products of humankind's ages-long string of sin and foolishness. People so easily blame God for their heartaches and disappointments rather than those who have messed the world up. A good God becomes the scapegoat. The guilty go free. Humankind messed up the world, but God gets the blame.

Suffering can indeed open people to deeper realities and to closer communion with God. But the door of suffering hangs on unusual hinges. It swings both ways. Suffering produces enormous spiritual benefits in people

33

WHAT MAKES THE
DOOR OF SUFFERING
SWING ONE WAY OR
THE OTHER?
SUGGEST SOME
PASSAGES WHERE
THE BIBLE SPEAKS TO
THIS QUESTION.

all over the world. But when we look at the amount of suffering flooding this earth, we are forced to admit that on the personal level at least, most suffering is good for nothing. It is wasted. Or worse, it turns many people away from God in bitterness and despair.

If suffering always generated growth and improvement in our hearts, then the world would be a far more beautiful place by now. We must reluctantly conclude that most of the deluge of bad stuff fails to touch people's souls for any good. God knocks at the door when people hurt. Most ignore the call to open up. Or else they fail to hear the One who alone can heal them. Some angrily push the caller away. A few do reach out. They are changed for good.

—

I will give you a new
heart and put a
new spirit in you;
I will remove from
you your heart of stone
and give you a
heart of flesh.

EZEKIEL 36:26

—

4

A SECOND LOOK AT SUFFERING

What does it mean to grow spiritually?

There may be endless ways to grow spiritually. The Bible describes necessary and desirable virtues, traits, goals, standards, and expectations in dozens of ways and words. Fundamentally, it boils down to loving God and people more. If that is so, then spiritual growth is the deepening and advancing of our relationships that spark us to do good works of all kinds.

Ernie lives around the corner from us. I expect to see him in heaven someday because Ernie loves Jesus. But when it comes to a broader practice of loving God, Ernie doesn't get it. Ernie drives a tow truck on the graveyard shift. When his duties end, around 6:00 A.M., he regularly picks up a meal of sorts at a fast-food outlet. Then he drives home and sits in front of his house, smoking and munching. When he's finished, he dumps his trash on the

DO YOU BUY THIS
DEFINITION OF
SPIRITUAL GROWTH?
EXPLAIN.

street, locks the truck, and heads for bed. Ernie's reverence for nature, an elementary spiritual step, doesn't exist.

WHAT KIND OF A JOLT DID IT TAKE IN YOUR LIFE TO MOVE YOU TO A HIGHER LEVEL OF FAITH?

Loving God fully includes a deep, wide, and inclusive sensitivity to living things. It includes our appreciation for beauty and harmony, and our intention to be responsible caretakers of creation. I wonder how much of a jolt it would take to move Ernie beyond nursery-school-level faith?

SUSTAINING PROGRESS

Growth that advances beyond kindergarten goodness requires continual guidance, consistent instruction, and the prayerful support of godly collaborators. The initial, painful shock that awakens complacent people may propel them closer to God. But without ongoing sustenance such spiritual progress soon slips away and dries up.

When Ben, her ninety-year-old downstairs buddy, died, Meghan Anderson, age two-and-a-half, received her initial immersion in spiritual realities. "Ben is in heaven with Jesus," her mother explained. "But his body is in the cemetery." A complex paradox quietly slipped into little Meghan's heart. Not long after this, Easter arrived. Ben's death had prepared the way for a meaningful connection between Jesus' death and resurrection and Ben's ongoing life. This was all explained to Meghan and absorbed by her, at a toddler's level. Real personal loss in this tot's life raised life's biggest question. Loving, careful, positive answers, with proper timely reinforcement, nourishes her soul more and more deeply as her life goes on. *Suffering* may not describe Meghan's condition fairly, but certainly, at a preschool level, her situation brought her dissonance and perplexity. Through it, spiritual growth commenced at a lovely level.

TANGIBLE SPIRITUALITY

Spiritual growth may seem mostly a subtle, subjective thing. Often it remains an inexpressible feeling that we try to define by words like peace, hope, security, confidence, and love. Often we find it hard to say exactly what we now know and feel.

But our enhanced spirituality must eventually become visible. It may show itself in varying ways: prayerfulness, concern for others, Bible study, advocacy, generosity, or an awakened sensitivity to beauty, pain, wastefulness, or time.

REFLECT ON JESUS' WORDS IN JOHN 15: 1-17. WHY MUST SPIRITUAL GROWTH BECOME VISIBLE?

True spirituality becomes tangible. Eventually Ernie must realize that trashing the street contradicts his love for God.

A teacher of the law once asked Jesus what it would take to attain the high quality of life that is required of God's children. Jesus replied, "Love the Lord your God with all your heart and with all your soul and with all your mind and with all your strength . . . (and) love your neighbor as yourself" (Mark 12: 30-31).

When we grow spiritually through suffering, we live out this all-encompassing formula at a deeper and more personal level than those who never experience life-renewing heartache. Love, in the form of appreciation, valuing, and compassion, seldom deepens unless we come eye to eye with the threat of loss. As the saying goes, "The mind focuses keenly when facing a firing squad."

BEYOND RAW PAIN

Ecclesiastes 1:18 reminds us that "with much wisdom comes much sorrow; the more knowledge, the more grief." Pain doesn't affect everybody in the same way. Animals do not grow from their suffering. They can hurt deeply from illness or injury. Loneliness, abandonment, loss of a mate or a master depresses them. It confuses them and probably brings them some kind of grief. But it is not a credible jump to claim that animals can process this distress into something thoughtfully positive. Hurt? Yes. Growth? Unlikely.

All human beings do have the basic potential to grow spiritually from disappointments and devastation. But not all possess the mental resources, vocabulary, and

41

insightfulness necessary to think about life below the surface. For many of us, hurt, loss, and tragedy stay on the level of raw pain. The only improvement in our condition comes from ordinary support systems and from the passage of time. Others of us choose to keep all that is sad or bad at a level below our active consciousness. That way we lessen the intense hurt we feel, but at the same time we cancel any real growth. Then we do not truly suffer. We merely hurt for a while.

CAN YOU GIVE EXAMPLES OF SUFFERING ON A DEEPER LEVEL? ALTHOUGH IT HURT MORE, WAS IT MORE USEFUL AS WELL? EXPLAIN.

The irony here is that education, thoughtfulness, and an informed spirituality probably set the stage for *deeper* suffering. The richer our inner person, the more profound our suffering may be. Children like Meghan Anderson do not really suffer because of their loss. Neither do thoughtless, shallow, ignorant people.

We should see suffering as more than feeling pain. If we define suffering carefully, we may have to give the franchise on this unwelcome commodity to thoughtful humans alone. Properly understood, suffering is tied to the capacity and willingness to think about things, to wonder about them, to reflect, to seek meanings, causes, and explanations.

SUFFERING THAT'S WELL THOUGHT OUT

The death of a child or a partner causes some kind of distress to every higher animal. Geese, for example, mate for life. If one falls to a hunter or some other enemy, the surviving goose grieves. Before finally flying on, the living mate searches for days, apparently with mournful longing. However, this is instinctive behavior, not contemplative mourning. Such animals do not suffer in the sense of enduring the heightened agony brought on by shattered memories and the painful realization that they must build a new life from scratch, and do so all alone. Nor are animals crushed by the injustice of it all, or maddened by an apparent divine letdown or the notion that God has double-crossed them. In the same way, people concerned primarily with the basic survival needs of food and shelter probably suffer less than those of us who have the time, thoughtfulness, and reflective tools for delving deeper.

This means that sheer pain by itself is not likely to produce spiritual growth in us. Suffering is necessary. We need to be able to think beyond the surface: to sense, feel, and reflect on the deeper significance and ramifications of our loss. If sheer pain provided a fertile environment for spiritual growth, we would have a far better world today. Pain is so prevalent and inevitable that it would be a sure thing.

Suffering only comes to thoughtful, sensitive, reflective souls. Because of this, they alone are equipped for spiritual deepening.

THE NEXT STEP

Because feeling pain precedes most spiritual growth, any system that largely anesthetizes away the pangs of distress and sorrow that ordinarily accompany our loss is counterproductive to our spiritual growth. Painlessness initiates little change for the better. Only wounded people who acutely and thoughtfully lament what has happened to them are likely to mobilize their resources to remedy or prevent any repetition of whatever awful circumstances led to their devastation. This is the next step in spiritual progress.

All of us possess a reservoir of emotions that stands ready to respond to the evils and accidents of this world. Sorrow, sympathy, compassion, and agony are easily triggered by deaths, injuries, injustices, and deprivations. When bad things happen, God's people must be moved by them. Their hearts must be touched.

Feeling distress for others or ourselves often triggers spiritual change for the better. The closer to home our hurt is, the greater the likelihood and the amount of spiritual improvement.

Widows and widowers constantly tell me that they never realized how helpful a phone call, a note, or a hug could be until their own spouse died and they found

READ PSALM 22 OR PSALM 88. DO SUCH PSALMS OF LAMENT SHOW A LACK OF SPIRITUALITY OR FAITH IN GOD? OR DO THEY REVEAL JUST THE OPPOSITE? EXPLAIN.

themselves bereft and alone. Now that they know this need from their own experience, it has become second nature to them to give out these small, meaningful gifts. Spiritual growth—tangible and helpful, rises from the ashes of their sorrow.

Mothers Against Drunk Driving (M.A.D.D.) is an international movement of hurt and angry people that has saved thousands of lives since its inception in the early seventies. These mothers have experienced the ultimate loss, the death of a child, as a result of an alcohol-impaired automobile driver. Their pain, now mobilized into world-improving action, changes laws, raises consciousness, and tightens penalties on drunk driving. Whether they call it that or not, this is God's Spirit at work. Good works always come from God.

NEW OPPORTUNITIES

Today the world offers the kinds of opportunities that were rare in past history. Individuals now can make a difference. We are not trapped in an unchangeable web. Our society is not so tightly controlled by tradition or circumstance that we can only cry out or grow bitter. Today, at least in the free world, we can direct our deep feelings toward causes, campaigns, movements, and projects that attack evil, discover solutions, change habits, and eliminate carelessness and callousness. Injured souls, sore and seething, make the best revolutionaries God can find.

The Spirit of God meets us in the wilderness of suffering, intending to breathe new life into our parched and desperate souls. That's why some of the great discoveries of science, classic works of art, heart-touching music, poetry, and literature have flowed out of the deserts of people's lives. Sad times create the most fertile environment for us to be open to the Spirit of God inspiring us, moving us, focusing our positive creativity like nothing and nobody else can.

Spiritual growth calls us one step further than we've gone in the past. Betty Ford, wife of President Gerald

Ford, found herself gripped tightly by the vise of chemical misuse. She frequently embarrassed herself and her husband by showing up at public occasions while severely impaired by drugs and alcohol. Providentially, help reached her muddled mind, and gradually she worked her way free to full sobriety. God met her in the process, calling her to use her fame and her pilgrimage to health to benefit others. The Betty Ford Center emerged from her wilderness. Enormous good now flows daily from her sad time in the swamp of addiction.

WHAT HAVE YOU SUFFERED THAT HAS SENSITIZED YOU TO THE NEEDS OF OTHERS WHO ARE IN THE SAME BOAT? HAVE YOU TAKEN THE NEXT STEP OF ACTUALLY DOING SOMETHING FOR THEM?

If we have a fatalistic attitude, we see bad circumstances as sent by God to teach, discipline, or punish us. We then logically conclude that they are God's will and that we should accept them quietly and passively. Such thinking defeats God's spirit of renewal. Certainly, as the pain lets up, we must learn, change, and repent in the wake of the painful events in our lives. But we should not accept bad things as inevitable and inalterable. God calls us to rage against evil. God calls us to initiate or support causes that aim to eradicate every enemy, from cancer to child abuse, drunk driving to thievery, clutter to chaos.

DYING FOR OTHERS

Spiritual growth may be most complete when our flattened souls have been dragged back to their feet, resuscitated by the Spirit of Christ, who defeated death, and energized by the Holy Spirit into servants who conduct world-bettering activities, projects, and campaigns. We find full spiritual maturity in people who are guided by the Spirit of Christ into a new form of altruistic suffering. This suffering is a kind of dying for others. These people sacrifice their own comfort as they direct their energies into entering the pain of others to change, modify, and lessen it. This is Christlikeness. We see it in such simple gifts as listening to another person's story or in fighting furiously against specific types of injustice or criminality.

John sets his alarm clock for 3:00 A.M. on Tuesday each week. He goes off while it's still dark to take phone calls from distressed souls who, for a few minutes, need the caring response of another human being. Some call with great pain. Others are lonely. A few are mentally ill. All touch John, test his wisdom, challenge his empathy, and stretch his love. For four hours each week, John leaves his comfortable bed to enter the pain and perplexity of total strangers. He hurts with them and for them. He questions, listens, suggests, and prays. Energized and exhausted, he then heads off for a full day of work.

IS THIS THE KIND OF "DYING" JESUS HAS IN MIND IN JOHN 12: 23-28? EXPLAIN.

This is a form of dying for others. John gives up his well-being to helplessly share another person's predicament. John gives up a sense of control and competence to wade into a pool of pain he cannot fix, control, or straighten out. He gives a lift to his dozen or so callers by sacrificing his feelings of safety and security in order to pay attention to their messes. That's a form of dying to which Christ calls us.

John's is the ripe spiritual fruit that God's Spirit can and does produce in us when we are touched by Jesus' love, moved by it to deny ourselves, take up our cross daily, and follow him (Luke 9:23).

—

Like one who takes
away a garment on a
cold day,
or like vinegar
poured on soda,
is one who sings songs
to a heavy heart.

—

WE WERE UNDER GREAT PRESSURE, FAR BEYOND OUR
ABILITY TO ENDURE, SO THAT WE DESPAIRED EVEN OF LIFE.
INDEED, IN OUR HEARTS WE FELT THE SENTENCE OF DEATH.

2 Corinthians 1:8-9

5

FAITH THAT NEEDS NOT KNOW

*What can we say to the wounded
that really helps them?*

Aspirins stand high on our list of God's helps for hurting people. Few of us advocate toughing out every headache or backache. There's not much good in sheer pain. Raw, relentless pain produces little more than grim endurance and despair.

But when the heartaches of life come along, aspirins won't do. The pat little answers well-meaning people hand out like over-the-counter painkilling tablets usually make the pain worse instead of better. Often they effectively silence the cries of the wounded. That's the real danger of these standard platitudes—they silence people while their hurt endures unspoken.

FROM YOUR OWN
EXPERIENCE, GIVE
SOME EXAMPLES OF
INSTANCES WHEN
PEOPLE HAVE
GLOSSED OVER DEEP
PAIN. HOW DID THAT
FEEL?

POWER TO GET BACK UP

God has created us with an amazing capacity for healing and for going on with life even in the wake of the most unbelievable wounds. I've already mentioned my two good friends who have lost teenaged sons to suicide. Another friend, Bob, buried his wife and three young children after they were smashed by a drunk driver on Halloween night. There was no God-ordained or God-allowed purpose or plan in this. No good lay hidden away in this travesty. It happened because of the sinful, careless drunkenness of a man. Yet today, ten years later, Bob's devastated soul—forever changed—again laughs, loves, and praises the Lord.

Nothing anyone quoted in the way of wise sayings, Bible texts, or cheerful proverbs moved Sharon, Shirley, or Bob forward. God just gradually dragged them to their feet and started them walking again. Faith, a caring and supportive Christian community, love, and a God-given capacity to overcome the impossible has nudged them back into life. "Healed" is not the right word. Broken legs heal. Bones return to the way they were—like new, maybe even stronger. But the death of one's children cannot be healed. Wounded forever, these parents are, nevertheless, back on their feet and moving. They go on. But always the deep wound is there. The pain can return instantly, in full strength, at any time. It's never gone once and for all. So "healed" is not the right word. But they do get up again. Joy, laughter, creativity, and love ring out and shine once more.

HOW DOES THE RECOVERY OF HURTING PEOPLE "COME FROM GOD"?

Their ongoing lives now look rich and productive. But their recovery comes from God, not from pious phrases dropped on them by friends. Their well-being may be attributed to prayer and encouragement, but not to pat answers. Those thoughtlessly chosen Scripture texts people quoted to them to help them heal probably slowed their recovery instead.

THREE ROADS

Devastated people enter a place reserved only for the suffering. Among other things, it's a place of trial and temptation. The supreme spiritual temptation occurs here at the junction to which our suffering inevitably leads us. At this crossroads we find three roads, not two. One road, chosen by many, is the way of bitterness and godlessness. Another road, equally crowded, is the road of "knowledge" and "understanding." This freeway is traveled by the multitudes of church-goers who have answers for why bad things happen. They spout high-sounding answers. They suggest pious solutions. They offer theological explanations for perplexing situations. They travel with God—at least, they think they do. In reality, by pretending to know all the answers, they are self-propelled and self-sufficient. They journey on, injured, but insulated from the full shot by their knowl-edge—knowledge like: "This was God's will"; "There was a purpose in this awfulness"; "It's all part of God's plan"; "This is all for the best."

That kind of knowledge puts a suffering person in the driver's seat on this road. Having answers has a way of sheltering and easing the pain. Randomness or senseless-ness is maddening. Having answers is a path every true Christian sufferer is sorely tempted to choose. Those who believe tragedy is in some way attributable to God, or allowed by God, are helping themselves to anesthesia. It lessens the hurt to believe that there is purpose to this sheer awfulness. To be "sure" in this way is to regain a sense of control. So this reluctance to leave things unan-swered tempts us all.

But then there is the third road. Here is the true "road less traveled." It is the way few take. Here most move slowly because they're on their knees. Ill-prepared, they struggle on with little in their hands and no answers on their lips. They simply follow Jesus, relinquishing con-trol to their Good Shepherd, not to their own logic and reasoning. Trusting Jesus, they stagger and stumble on.

IS THIS REAL KNOWLEDGE? EITHER WAY, IS IT HELPFUL TO A SUFFERING PERSON?

They are the ones of whom Jesus said, "My sheep listen to my voice; I know them, and they follow me. I give them eternal life, and they shall never perish; no one can snatch them out of my hand" (John 10:27-28).

FAITH THAT DOES NOT KNOW

The "road less traveled" is the way of faith that lacks specific answers and understanding beyond the obvious recognition of human error. Pilgrims with such faith see things differently. Their tear-filled eyes somehow see a caring Jesus, a suffering Savior, who hurts with them. They have no pious or theological ideas that explain everything. They just know and feel deep loss, acute pain, and dreadful sorrow. For support and sustenance they reach out to the Lord with empty hands and cry out with faltering lips. They lack answers, but they find consolation in the companionship of the God who walks with them and weeps with them.

They are also hurt, angry, and confused. But they cling as best they can to the ancient promises of God—promises such as: "I will never leave you or forsake you." People like these are on the path of faith. It's the path Sarah and Abraham traveled: "By faith Abraham, when called to go . . . obeyed and went, even though he did not know where he was going. By faith he made his home in the promised land" (Heb. 11: 8-9).

The Old Testament narrative tells us that Job is blasted again and again with unimaginably horrific losses. Nevertheless, both he and his friends respond with streams of unwavering knowledge about all that has taken place. They disagree with each other, but each speaks confidently with a personal perspective on how to understand these devastating tragedies. Finally God speaks. God is irritated with all of them. Extolling the wonders and mysteries of creation, God challenges them to explain all those marvelous things. The implicit reprimand to them is this: "Who do you think you are to carry on as if you understand why bad things happen?"

Job gets the point: "I am unworthy—how can I reply to you? I put my hand over my mouth. I spoke once, but I have no answer—twice, but I will say no more" (Job 40: 4-5).

The family and fortunes of Job are only restored when he repents of his knowing attitude, prays for his friends, and simply trusts the Lord.

DOES JOB EVER FIND OUT WHY THESE TERRIBLE THINGS HAD TO HAPPEN? IS THAT THE RULE OR THE EXCEPTION?

AN ILL WIND THAT BLOWS NO GOOD

For some people the medicine of pat answers and brief proof texts is essential for temporary survival. Blunting the pain this way may enable them to get through another day. But numbness stops growth. They must eventually allow their pain to bite and sting badly enough to produce the helplessness that prepares them to meet God anew and follow Jesus in simple faith.

We must acknowledge that sometimes people deal with the kind of affliction that cannot be channeled into anything positive. Look at Gordon, for instance. After a moderately satisfying career in the banking business, Gordon retired. He looked forward to an active but satisfying life gardening, golfing, and grandparenting. After a few years of this, for no known reason, Gordon slipped into a deep, dark depression. All treatments have failed. Gordon, in his early seventies, sits or paces in his private torture chamber. To him this illness is just bad. It is good for nothing. There is no way he can recycle this hellish condition into spiritual growth or anything else of worth. Maybe someone else can. A family member or friend, possibly the frustrated psychiatrist or other professional helpers, may salvage some good from it. But, for Gordon, his depression hangs there like a cloud of unredeemable evil.

A quick glance around our globe and a walk back in history turn up enormous piles of terrible suffering that elude every attempt to make sense out of them. They offer not the least bit of benefit to their victims. The only thread of value that we can salvage from these events is the good, deep pain they trigger in those who

SO WHAT CAN WE
SAY TO HELP THOSE
WHO SUFFER
TERRIBLY AND
WITHOUT APPARENT
REASON?

stand at a safe distance from the victims. The sins of apartheid, the horrors of the holocaust, and the genocide in Rawanda quickly come to mind. For the immediate victims, these atrocities only bring raw badness. With time and effort and God's guidance, it remains for the rest of humanity to squeeze benefits from these evils. And that they must. Otherwise death wins.

Then Job replied . . .
"You asked, 'Who is this
that obscures my counsel
without knowledge?'
Surely I spoke of
things I did not
understand, things too
wonderful for me
to know."

JOB 42:1, 3

6

GODLY RESPONSE TO THE WOUNDEDNESS OF OTHERS

What is the crucial, first thing that those devastated by loss, injury, or oppression must do?

Not long ago my married daughter became mysteriously ill. A variety of strange and disturbing symptoms plagued her day after day. She dragged herself to her teaching job, struggled through the day, and then crashed in tears and misery when she finally made it home. Finally, one Saturday morning, her husband telephoned us to say that there was no change, no improvement. "Is there anything we can do?" Linda, my wife, agonized.

"Just pray. Just pray," Kevin suggested.

My wife Linda, a helpless mom two thousand miles away from our daughter, immediately and fervently acted on this suggestion. Then came a surprise. In less than an hour the phone rang again. "We think the problem is solved. After I talked with you a while ago, it suddenly dawned on me to check the prescription bottle of the pills Julie has been taking [for an unrelated condition]. They're the wrong ones! The pharmacy gave her somebody else's medicine!"

Prayer answered. In twenty-four hours Julie was fine.

MANY PEOPLE WOULD CALL THAT COINCIDENCE, NOT ANSWERED PRAYER. OTHERS WOULD CALL IT PROVIDENCE. WHAT DO YOU THINK? IS THERE SUCH A THING AS COINCIDENCE IN GOD'S WORLD?

NOTHING NEW

Time and again in Bible history we read that the people of God are in trouble and they cry out to God. Again and again God hears their cries as they make their impact. Our tears and groans move God to change things. When God's people were harshly enslaved, God answered their cries with a plan to lead them to a better place. It took a lot of time and effort, and even more suffering on their part. But God heard their cry and delivered them.

We find another very striking example of God's responsiveness in 2 Kings 20. It involves Hezekiah, the king of Israel, who had fallen ill and was at the point of death. The prophet Isaiah comes to him with this message: "This is what the LORD says: Put your house in order, because you are going to die; you will not recover" (2 Kings 20:1).

Naturally this hits the king very hard. The pronouncement breaks his heart. But he doesn't meekly accept the verdict. "Hezekiah turned his face to the wall and prayed to the LORD, 'Remember, O LORD, how I have walked before you faithfully and with wholehearted devotion and have done what is good in your eyes" (vv. 2-3).

Those were his words. Then came the tears. "And Hezekiah wept bitterly" (v. 3).

Surprisingly, within minutes, Isaiah is back with a second message from the Lord: "I have heard your prayer and seen your tears; I will heal you . . . I will add fifteen years to your life" (vv. 5-6).

There is a strong principle here, a pattern that we need to follow today. In our distress and pain the Lord is touched by our cries. We must cry out. If change is to occur, we must let our hearts roar. God not only heard the king's reasoning, but God was also moved by his tears. The almighty God listened to his claim and was touched by the king's powerful emotion, which he accented with tears.

CAN WE CHANGE GOD'S MIND? ABOUT THE PLAN OF SALVATION? ABOUT EVERYDAY STUFF?

SHORT-CIRCUITING THE HEALING PROCESS

A young woman had shared with a small group, somewhat tearfully, the story of her youth. Abuse and flagrant mistreatment by her father dominated her account. As she came to the end of her sad tale, another person broke in: "You have to forgive him and put it all behind you, you know."

Silence. The young woman politely nodded in response but no one else said anything. Finally I spoke to the forgiveness advocate. "Have you had experience with forgiving something like that?"

No, she had not, she admitted. I think she caught the intent of my inquiry. I was trying to say gently that unless you've been there, be slow to speak and hesitant to give advice. Neither I nor anyone else questioned the appropriateness of forgiveness as part of the eventual dissolving of this awful web of injury. But the way the topic of forgiveness was broached and its timing were completely wrong. Her advisor was intent on silencing the wounded one. She didn't want to hear about her pain or feel it. She rushed forward with insensitive theological advice, hoping that it would quickly dismiss the topic.

To do better, we should consider at least four steps.

STEP 1: FEEL THE PAIN

The first step in offering a compassionate response goes like this: When people entrust us with something as sensitive as their deep hurts, we must really try to feel their pain. After the manner of our Lord, we must truly hear their cry. That's where we find God in relation to our own plight. God is touched and feels our pain. And

WHY DOES IT HELP PEOPLE WHEN WE FEEL THEIR PAIN?

that's how we should react too. We shouldn't say or do anything else before we somehow imagine or remember or feel at least something of the suffering person's perplexity or pain. We must expend every effort to identify before we qualify to respond.

STEP 2: EMPATHIZE

The second step of offering a compassionate response asks us to clearly communicate in word or deed that we have been touched, smashed, or bewildered by the pain we discover in the person who is hurting. Our most articulate reaction may be just a heartfelt groan, as our own tears well up in our eyes. It could be a tender, silent embrace. Whatever it is, it must clearly communicate that we feel their pain.

Recently I shared with a friend my weariness over conducting three funerals in five days. His response left me cold: "You chose this kind of work, didn't you?" His response came through to me like this: "Quit complaining or change professions."

Later, someone else showed me some empathy and understanding: "It must be draining to walk with so many grieving people in such a short time span." That helped. She heard my cry and let me know she understood. A spirit-lifting dose of empathy lifted me a little in the direction I needed to go.

STEP 3: HELP THEM CRY

IDENTIFY SOME OF THESE PLATITUDES THAT STOP A SUFFERING PERSON FROM POURING OUT GRIEF.

The third step prompts us to allow and enable the injured one to cry out. But more than that, we should cry out with them on their behalf. We should not purposely or inadvertently silence their cries. We do better to say nothing and endure the awkwardness of wordlessness than to relieve our own discomfort by mouthing platitudes. While we intend such words to be helpful, they actually silence the injured one, causing him or her to fall silent.

The Scriptures contain a multitude of "crying out" passages. God's people often raise their voices in gut-wrenching protest to God. There are actually more psalms of lament than there are psalms dealing with any other theme. They are the cries of those suffering deeply and feeling abandoned by God. Clearly the Holy Spirit intends us to see and use these models as instruments of healing in reacting to the wrongs and spiritual loneliness that comes into our lives.

Here are just a few examples gleaned from the psalms of lament.

HOW WOULD YOU ANSWER THE BUDDING THEOLOGIAN WHO OBJECTS TO THESE LAMENTS, NOTING THAT GOD IS ALWAYS PRESENT EVERYWHERE?

> *My God, my God, why have you forsaken me?*
>> *Why are you so far from saving me,*
>> *so far from the words of my groaning?*
> *O my God, I cry out by day, but you do not answer,*
>> *by night, and am not silent.*
>>> —PSALM 22:1-2

> *In God we make our boast all day long,*
>> *and we will praise your name forever.*
> *But now you have rejected and humbled us . . .*
>> *You gave us up to be devoured like sheep . . .*
> *Awake, O LORD! Why do you sleep?*
>> *Rouse yourself! Do not reject us forever.*
> *Why do you hide your face*
>> *and forget our misery and oppression?*
>>> —PSALM 44:8-9, 11, 23-24

> *I cry to you for help, O LORD . . .*
> *Why, O LORD, do you reject me*
>> *and hide your face from me?*
>>> —PSALM 88:13-14

God does not respond to our stony, distress-denying silence. But when we express our grief, God hears our cries and comes closer and heals us. As God's people we are called to feel the pain of our friends—to allow and encourage them to groan their protests. With them we must call out in dismay to the Lord, and join them in their laments. This can only happen through the kind of faith that trusts in a God who hears, is touched, cares and responds with a healing, strengthening, comforting presence.

In Psalm 18 we observe how David talked to God: "I call to the LORD, who is worthy of praise, and I am saved from my enemies" (v. 3). Then, in verse six, he adds, "In my distress I called to the LORD; I cried to my God for help. . . . he heard my voice; my cry came before him, into his ears."

Again and again we read how God's people cried out to God when they were defeated, depressed, and despairing. Our cries must ring out today as theirs did so many years ago. Compassionate friends enhance rather than inhibit this part of our healing process. A truly healthy relationship with God emerges when, while reverently worshiping God, we boldly protest our objections to the way things are. Then we'll discover that God accepts our hurt and anger more readily than he accepts our sweet passivity.

WHAT MAKES IT SO HARD FOR US TO GIVE THIS KIND OF FITTING RESPONSE?

Earlier in this chapter we listened in as an untimely spokesperson urged an injured woman to forgive. Following the steps of compassionate response we've examined, she might instead have tried one of the following: tears, a hug, a touch, and then a simple comment such as, "Oh, that is so sad. That makes me so angry. What a terrible thing—your own father!"

Empathy enhances spiritual growth. Love cries out on behalf of another person. What the person who suffered abuse needed was a prayer that screamed to God of the injustice done to her in her childhood and a plea for God's healing presence to work in her life.

STEP 4: LISTEN, AND LISTEN HARD

There is still another step we need to take in showing a compassionate response. We must invite the injured one to tell us all they can about what happened. Of course, our invitation to share in detail can only appear genuine and be effective when we show that we're really ready to listen actively and energetically. We need to make appropriate eye contact. We need to assume a posture that reaches out to the person to whom we're listening. It takes self-discipline not to interrupt, change the subject, or give superficial advice. But all of this is only a sequel to the initial need for crying out boldly and lamenting with all our heart to God.

When devastated, struggling people receive genuine, warmhearted understanding from friends, God's presence and love become more real and meaningful. Good friends acting on God's behalf strongly nourish spiritual growth in those who hurt. That nurture includes vehement dialogue with God from the depths of their souls, dialogue that is understood and accepted by caring listeners, who in turn cry out to God their own rendition of the suffering person's lament. When we willingly and lovingly walk with people in their pain and help them express it, we can move along with them into asking the tough questions they face. We'll examine some of those in the next chapter.

DESCRIBE THE SPIRITUAL GROWTH THAT CARING FRIENDS BRING ABOUT IN SUFFERING PEOPLE.

When Jesus saw her
weeping . . . he was
deeply moved in spirit
and troubled. . . .
Jesus wept.

JOHN 11:33-35

NOW THE DWELLING OF GOD IS WITH MEN,
AND HE WILL LIVE WITH THEM. THEY WILL BE HIS PEOPLE,
AND GOD HIMSELF WILL BE WITH THEM AND BE THEIR GOD.
HE WILL WIPE EVERY TEAR FROM THEIR EYES.
THERE WILL BE NO MORE DEATH OR MOURNING
OR CRYING OR PAIN.

Revelation 21:3-4

7

WHERE IS GOD IN ALL THIS PAIN?

*When tragedy, illness, or loss strike,
where is God? Causing it?
Allowing it? Watching helplessly?*

Several years ago two separate and seemingly distant pieces of my life's puzzle snapped together to make a fresh picture for me. One piece emerged from the book of Genesis that I was studying at the time, the other from a major world news story.

OUR GRIEVING GOD

The news story was of an unprecedented, ugly oil spill near Valdez, Alaska. It wreaked havoc with the ocean and every living thing in, on, and around it.

The Scripture passage was a relatively obscure verse, Genesis 6:6, written in the context of the wickedness into which humankind had fallen so shortly after its good creation. The part that hit me was the description of the

Lord's emotions in response to this sad situation: "The LORD was grieved . . . and his heart was filled with pain."

HOW CLOSELY CAN GOD IDENTIFY WITH OUR GRIEF AND PAIN? DOES GOD KNOW WHAT IT'S LIKE TO BE BETRAYED OR TO LOSE A CHILD?

Suddenly the two pieces clicked together for me. Of course! It was so obvious, but I'd never seen it before: that's how God feels about the oil spill too. God loves creation, and this damage grieves and pains God. The transition in my mind to human suffering was immediate and natural. If God's heart breaks over such wanton injury to creation, how much more must it break over human suffering and devastation?

GOD GRIEVES WITH US

It wasn't long after this that I heard myself say to a mother, who was grieving the death of her young son, that "the Lord is weeping with you." She was not in an analytic or questioning frame of mind so she just let that image of holy empathy flow into her troubled spirit and comfort her. In many weeks of listening and talking, this was probably the most helpful sentence I had expressed.

READ PHILIPPIANS 2:6-8. WHAT KIND OF A GOD DOES THIS PASSAGE PORTRAY— ONE WHO REMAINS PLEASANTLY ALOOF FROM OUR PAIN?

I believe that figure of speech. It conveys an accurate impression of our Lord's relationship to us in troublesome times. It fits with that brief glimpse into God's heart that we find in Genesis 6:6. It also conforms to the spirit of Jesus, which is so passionately with us and for us in his life, death, and resurrection.

GOD ATTACKED

A chaplain friend told me this story, a dramatic vignette from his life as a psychiatric pastor. A young woman patient on the hospital ward came daily to his Spiritual Life class. She had a standoffish manner but regularly raised the same question in a taunting manner: "Chaplain, where was your God when I was raped by my uncle, time and again? Where was God then?"

The chaplain didn't know how to answer this agonizing question. His conventional responses felt shallow, superficial, and even wrong. So he tried his best to convey an attitude of kindly sympathy. But words failed him.

Then one day the young woman arrived in class with a different look on her face. The defiance was gone, and she radiated peace. When time came for group sharing, she quickly spoke up. "Chaplain," she said, "I have the answer to my question. It came to me last night as I was lying on my bed. It was almost like someone was talking to me. I know it was God. God said, 'I was with you every time you were raped. I was raped with you. When your uncle attacked you, he attacked me.'"

Knowing that about God healed her spirit immensely. Realizing that God identified with her in her suffering instead of standing apart made all the difference in the world to her.

DOES THIS IMPLY THAT GOD IS WEAK AND HELPLESS? EXPLAIN.

IDENTIFICATION

As they talked further, the chaplain accepted her revelation. It changed and strengthened him as well. In fact, this wounded woman's discovery revolutionized his whole way of thinking.

Together they found specific Bible verses that touchingly supported their new understanding, passages they had never seen in this wonderful way. They read about Jesus pointing to a time of reckoning when the Lord will paint an unmistakably clear picture about his total identification with his children. Matthew 25:40 clearly taught that when people do anything caring and helpful for God's children, they do it for God himself. Conversely, when we damage God's people, we damage God—so closely does the Lord identify with us.

Our Lord also strongly emphasizes this unity with even the smallest and weakest:

IF A LITTLE CHILD HURTS, DO HIS OR HER PARENTS AND SIBLINGS HURT TOO? DOES THAT EXPLAIN JESUS' POINTED THREAT IN VERSE SIX?

"And whoever welcomes a little child like this in my name welcomes me. But if anyone causes one of these little ones who believe in me to sin, it would be better for him to have a large millstone hung around his neck and to be drowned in the depths of the sea."

—MATTHEW 18:5-6

FROM THE BEGINNING

The message of these passages and of the whole Bible is one of the Lord's total love, concern, and identification with humankind. We're far better off, and much closer to the truth, when we see God as feeling our pain, being brokenhearted with us and burdened by our plight. That's much better than to point to God as somehow allowing it or even causing it. Jesus said, "I was hungry and you gave me something to eat, I was thirsty and you gave me something to drink, I was a stranger and you invited me in, . . . I was sick and you looked after me" (Matt. 25:35-36).

Biblical revelation presents a gracious Creator in love with his creatures, a God who cares deeply about the messes and tragedies we have created for each other and ourselves. The problems of this life, great and small, are of human, not divine, origin. God made the world perfect, and the breakage is the evidence and outcome of sin and foolishness in people. It is not from God. In light of our selfishness and carelessness since the beginning of history, it seems the height of ignorance and irresponsibility to directly or indirectly blame God for our suffering. People have messed up God's world, not God.

IS IT IMPORTANT FOR US TO KNOW THE ORIGIN OF OUR HURT? EXPLAIN. GIVE SOME EXAMPLES FROM YOUR OWN LIFE OR FROM THE LIFE OF SOMEONE CLOSE TO YOU.

It's true that the Bible does speak of bad circumstances developing as the result of God's punishment, discipline, or permission. And sometimes our sorrows originate in the devil. But in our own lives we do not receive such information about origins. All we know about is the obvious—human failure, genetic breakdown, personal carelessness, natural disasters, criminal behavior, accidents, inherited traits. That's what make bad things happen.

But we also know the Lord cares and hurts along with us. And he heals and helps us to get up again, to grow, and to find ways of becoming more than we were before the bad stuff hit us. In the process, we must face our grief and express it openly and honestly. We'll take that subject up in chapter 8.

—

*"Blessed are you
who weep now,
for you will laugh."*

LUKE 6:21

—

> "BLESSED ARE THOSE WHO MOURN,
> FOR THEY WILL BE COMFORTED."
>
> *Matthew 5:4*

8

THE PRIMARY SOURCE OF SUFFERING

However big or small, which losses still distress you right now?

Losses cause grief. Grief can hurt like a gaping wound and sicken us like a terrible plague. The loss of anything or anybody we love or really care about triggers grief. And loss in our lives—expected or shockingly unexpected—is inevitable. Because it is, it often presents us with the primary challenge that ushers in a spiritual revolution—either for the good or for the bad.

CAN YOU GIVE EXAMPLES FROM YOUR EXPERIENCE? WAS THE CHANGE ALWAYS GOOD OR BAD, OR DID YOU SOMETIMES SEE MIXED RESULTS? EXPLAIN.

Our capacity and willingness to care and connect with people, pets, places, objects, conditions, hopes, and dreams sets the stage for eventual grief. In fact, all of life is a continuous process of moving on from one love to another, always leaving behind something or someone whom we have valued and cherished.

MOVING ON

Consider the human fetus after nine months of life inside its mother. Now if it had to make a choice, do you think it would decide to stay or move ahead with birth? I think it would stay. Why struggle and hurt to leave? Right where it is, the fetus enjoys a perfect environment: always warm, food without effort, no bright lights, no loud sounds, no insecure handling. It lives in a safe, convenient paradise. To go on and out brings a life of crying for help, uncertainty, hunger, chilliness, handling, and hurting. Still, such a choice for comfort would lead to death. It's the difficult way that leads to life.

FROM YOUR OWN EXPERIENCE, PROVIDE SOME EXAMPLES OF HOW "GROWTH AND DISCOMFORT WALK HAND IN HAND."

All of life copies this pattern. Growth and discomfort walk hand in hand. Necessary changes and losses season our lives from start to finish. Most of the time we feel the pinch, cry briefly our lament, and keep growing. But when we're stunned by unexpected or untimely grief, we stop in our tracks, at least for a while.

The losses that really knock us down, throw us backwards, and usher in whole seasons of suffering are those that knock out the pillars of our lives, the supports that give us joy and security, the ones we rely and lean on. Usually these are beloved family members or friends. Death is a consistent culprit, but often divorce or other circumstances steal people away from us as well. Whatever these circumstances are, they always brings grief.

TYPES OF LOSS

Numerous other hurtful losses can seriously trouble us, cause prolonged sadness, and even trigger depression. They include

HAVE YOU EXPERIENCED THESE KINDS OF LOSSES? HOW DID THEY AFFECT YOU?

- deterioration of health
- physical or mental impairment
- death of a pet
- loss of independence or freedom
- loss of valuable property
- amputations and surgical loss of physical functions
- loss of a sense of control due to burglary, robbery, or rape

- job loss or obligatory retirement
- departure or delinquency of children
- moving, change of residence
- death of a dream, hope, or plan
- breaking a relationship or friendship
- fire, earthquake, tornado, or other natural disasters
- birth of a physically or mentally impaired child

BIBLICAL GRIEF

The stories of the Bible abound with accounts of loss and grief. They range from God's own brokenheartedness over a spoiled creation to Jesus' weeping over the spiritual mistakenness of Jerusalem, from the grief of David over the death of Absalom to that of the Israelites crying over their exile. The grief of Job is classic. So too are the lamentations of Jeremiah. The book of Psalms is replete with the cries of disappointed and swindled people.

The Bible speaks to grieving people in all ages and places, because so many biblical characters in so many different circumstances cry out with heartache and sorrow that are credible and understandable. Their humanness touches ours.

Here are just some of the many examples we find in the Old Testament.

AS YOU SURVEY THIS LIST, PUT YOURSELF INTO THE STORY. HOW WOULD YOU HAVE GRIEVED THESE EVENTS IF THEY HAD HAPPENED TO YOU?

- When his wife died, "Abraham went to mourn for Sarah and to weep over her" (Gen. 23:2).
- When Esau finds that he was tricked out of both his birthright and his father's blessing, "Esau wept aloud" (Gen. 27:38).
- Jacob is falsely told that Joseph, his son, has been killed. "Then Jacob tore his clothes, put on sackcloth and mourned for his son many days. . . . he refused to be comforted" (Gen. 37:34-35).
- When Jacob dies, Joseph reacts: "Joseph threw himself upon his father and wept over him and kissed him" (Gen. 50:1).
- "When the whole community learned that Aaron had died, the entire house of Israel mourned for him thirty days" (Num. 20:29).

- When Jephthah rashly vowed to sacrifice his daughter, she responded, "But grant me this one request. . . . Give me two months to roam the hills and weep with my friends, because I will never marry" (Judg. 11:37).
- When they find their hometown ravaged by an enemy, "David and his men wept aloud until they had no strength left to weep" (1 Sam. 30:4).
- David laments the deaths of Saul and Jonathan: "They mourned and wept and fasted till evening" (2 Sam. 1:12).
- After being raped, David's granddaughter, Tamar, "put ashes on her head and tore the ornamented robe she was wearing. She put her hand on her head and went away, weeping aloud as she went" (2 Sam. 13:19).

GRIEF IN THE NEW TESTAMENT

The New Testament also gives us many examples of grieving people.

- Matthew describes the grief caused by Herod's slaughter of the baby boys of Bethlehem by quoting the prophet Jeremiah:

> *A voice is heard in Ramah,*
> *weeping and great mourning,*
> *Rachel weeping for her children*
> *and refusing to be comforted,*
> *because they are no more.*
>
> —MATTHEW 2:18

- Mary, her friends, and Jesus all grieve the death of Lazarus: "When Jesus saw her weeping, and the Jews who had come along with her also weeping, he was deeply moved in spirit and troubled. . . . Jesus wept. Then the Jews said, 'See how he loved him!'" (John 11:33-36).
- Mary Magdalene weeps at Jesus' tomb: "[the angels] asked her, 'Woman, why are you crying?' 'They

have taken my Lord away,' she said, 'and I don't know where they have put him'" (John 20:13).

- Paul grieves for those who refuse the gospel: "For, as I have often told you before and now say again even with tears, many live as enemies of the cross of Christ" (Phil. 3:18).

OPEN TO GRIEF

Our brief survey demonstrates that the Scriptures hold before us a realistic and natural attitude about responding to disappointment, death of a loved one, and other painful circumstances. The people of the Bible, including Jesus himself, are passionate and open with sorrow and sadness. They express outwardly, visibly, and dramatically the inner pain of their distressed and broken hearts. They are not inhibited by moralistic constraints that demand that they remain calm, reserved, and accepting of sad affairs. Even though they prove their mettle by facing terror with resolve and steadfastness, they openly show their grief.

Spiritual maturity cannot be gauged on the basis of how stoically or frantically we handle a crisis. Spiritual growth does not express itself by forcing us to dry our tear ducts and stifle our lamentations and cries. As Christian friends of people who grieve, we ought to avoid praising and celebrating their tearlessness and phony cheeriness.

In fact, we can infer quite the opposite from Scripture. Normal, healthy children of God reside in a safe harbor of friendship with the Lord that frees them to express themselves vehemently, forcefully, and explosively. Securely embraced by their loving God, they know that their natural, personal feelings are acceptable and normal, whatever they might be.

WHICH APPROPRIATE FORMS OF GRIEVING HAVE YOU SEEN? HAVE YOU SEEN INAPPROPRIATE ONES?

SETTING THE STAGE

In Old Testament history, Naomi stands out as a faithful, God-loving woman. When she's hit with her husband's death, she bursts out with a surprising litany of anger and bitterness, "The Almighty has made my life very bitter. I went away full, but the Lord has brought me back empty" (Ruth 1:20-21).

Job also stands out as someone who can grieve openly and complain loudly, even though God himself boasts that Job is "blameless and upright" (Job 1:8). After a long series of major losses, Job cries out, "May the day of my birth perish, and the night it was said, 'A boy is born!' That day—may it turn to darkness" (Job 3:3-4).

WHAT ARE THE BEST WAYS OF TEACHING CHILDREN TO COPE APPROPRIATELY WITH GRIEF?

Through early teaching and training, biblical examples such as these help us to set the stage for healthy and wholesome response to disaster and loss. They demonstrate over and over again how open God is to our deepest and strongest feelings. God understands. God accepts us. God responds to our cries whether we bend over with bitterness or meekly whimper in our weakness. Graciously, he even responds when we stoically keep our hurts bottled up inside.

However, spiritual growth progresses best when we are highly conscious of our dissonance. Living in denial, apathetically, or with an all-encompassing cheeriness in every dire circumstance short-circuits growth, maintains the status quo, and blocks the regenerative work of the Holy Spirit. Only when we allow ourselves to face our grief and express it, can we turn to God in prayer that's earnest, honest, and open. In chapter 9 we'll take a closer look at that kind of prayer.

We do not know what
we ought to pray for,
but the Spirit himself
intercedes for us with
groans that
words cannot express.

ROMANS 8:26

AND THE PRAYER OFFERED IN FAITH WILL MAKE THE SICK
PERSON WELL. . . . THE PRAYER OF A RIGHTEOUS MAN IS
POWERFUL AND EFFECTIVE.

James 5:15-16

9

PRAYER, A POTENT MEDICINE

*We often hear it said that God
answers prayer. What does that mean?*

She woke up shivering cold with a dozen daggers digging at her chest. She was in the recovery room. Surgery was over. The pain defied description. A guardian of orderliness stonewalled her feeble plea for medication. "Not yet," she snapped. Then a phrase drifted into the patient's anesthesia-clouded mind: "the power of prayer." Or was it "the power of praise"? She couldn't remember later exactly which final word finished the sentence, but either one fit. The words floated in from somewhere unknown and then dissipated along with her pain. Like a cleansing stream the four fresh words washed the pain away. Soon the knives of pain sliced once more, but again the mysterious spiritual morphine trickled in: "the power of prayer (praise)." And the sharp, cutting agony left as the words slipped away.

GIVE EXAMPLES OF
TIMES IN YOUR LIFE
WHEN GOD
ANSWERED YOUR
PRAYER, OR THE
PRAYER OF OTHERS
FOR YOU, WITH A
RESOUNDING "YES."
THINK ALSO OF
TIMES WHEN GOD
SAID "NO."

Linda and I both knew that scores, maybe even hundreds, of people were praying for her on this Good Friday, as her breast cancer surgery was underway. So interpreting this surprising, special, pain-killing phenomenon, we naturally leaned toward seeing it as prayer tangibly working. The prayers of caring friends floated powerfully over hundreds and thousands of miles, through walls, over mountains, around every obstacle, into her wounded body—lifting, healing, refreshing, and dissolving her pain.

HEALING PRAYER

One year has passed since the initial diagnosis. Surgery, chemotherapy, and reconstruction have battered Linda. But we both feel, and freshly believe, the prayers of concerned allies have carried her in an amazing way. The year goes down in the annals of our lives as a very good time in our history, not a dismal and wretched one. The spirit-lifting, body-benefitting power of God-directed intercession and of caring people sending multitudes of healing words and symbols of their love deserve the major credit.

HOW DOES PRAYER
HAVE SUCH A
POWERFUL EFFECT?
IS IT LIKE MAGIC?
IS ITS POWER
PSYCHOSOMATIC?

I confess, with some embarassment, to counting her "get well" cards. Over five hundred arrived in the mail. Nearly all of them included a handwritten inscription such as "You are in our prayers" or "We're praying for you." Those words, once innocuous in our experience, now stand with the finest gifts. By contrast, the kindly message "You're in our thoughts" felt cool and empty. We've come to understand that prayer activates and sends something good from God for the recipient in need. Just to be "in our thoughts" feels powerless. Prayer enhances healing, accelerates recovery, reduces pain, lessens complications, elevates a sense of well-being, pacifies the panicky, and saves lives. Neglecting to pray for downed souls seriously deprives them and cheats them out of potent spiritual medicine.

A TRIANGLE OF HEALING

Today I envision prayer in a triangular form. I have a mental picture of sending a prayer up to God on some-one's behalf. That line represents one leg of the triangle. Simultaneously the bottom line of the triangle extends from myself to the person being prayed for. From the peak of the triangle, where I place God, a line flows down from God to the individual I'm concerned about. This line is the stream of God's healing Spirit. But at the same time, as strength flows down from God, God is also communicating vital sustenance horizontally directly through me. As I hold the person in mind, I believe God's lifting grace, peace, and strength flow from me. I am more than an intercessor. As our reservoir of health, God uses our visualizing of the person in need and aims and dispatches our healing arrows directly to them.

The stories of blessed people like Linda, buoyed up by prayer, nourish hungry souls. Prayer is a practice that has survived over many centuries because of biblical exam-ples and instructions. But it is reinvigorated regularly by the stirring anecdotes, quiet reports, and sometimes stunning experiences of those who are injured and ill.

CONFIRMED RESULTS

Still more support now flows from modern-day research. Carefully conducted scientific experiments bear out the claims of God's prayerful disciples. The most zealous and steadfast Christians find little need for sci-entific proof of the power of prayer. They pray now, and always will, simply because the Bible tells them to. That's all they need. But not all stand where these spiri-tual redwoods do. Others find their energy and enthusi-asm strongly renewed by the positive conclusions of sci-entific research on the healing efficacy of prayer.

The best-known study involved one hundred and forty cardiac patients in a San Francisco hospital. Seventy were prayed for intensively by individuals out-side the hospital. Conventional treatment with no spe-cial prayer covered the others. Neither group was aware

IT WOULD BE INTERESTING TO DETERMINE IF IT WAS THE ACT OF PRAYER OR THE OBJECT OF PRAYER THAT MADE THE DIFFERENCE. DO YOU THINK IT WOULD MAKE A DIFFERENCE WHICH GOD WAS ADDRESSED IN THESE PRAYERS? EXPLAIN.

of the prayer program in process. The results remarkably demonstrated the positive benefits of spiritual intercession. Those who received it experienced earlier discharges, less painkillers, and fewer deaths.

Another set of experiments stretch our credulity but can inspire anyway. These involved common rye seeds. The goal was to determine if prayer or prayerlike processes could influence the rate of their germination. Sure enough, "prayed-for" seeds sprang to life more quickly than those left to follow nature's usual course. What's more, when seeds were stressed or sickened by a salt-water soak, they responded to prayer even more remarkably. It was as if prayer were especially powerful when the weak were targeted. These experiments provoke thought and awe, if not faith. Perhaps God reserves research like this for those who trust science to strengthen their weak faith.

DIFFERENT KINDS OF HEALING

A strong, clear, and reassuring message permeates Scripture. It may be summed up in this way: "God feels our pain, is touched deeply by our cries, and responds positively." Today we know, in thrilling, invigorating ways, that prayer improves every dismal situation. And the more prayer the better. Our well-being is strongly enhanced in all instances by the caring community promising and delivering a steady flow of intercession.

George Derr, for whom many were praying, recently called me for a pastoral visit to his hospital room. George had been knocked down by heart failure, and his future appeared radically revised. A long-time, active church member, George wanted to tell me about something that happened to him. Getting quickly to the point, he stated that "at 7:05 on January 6, I became a born-again Christian."

"Wow!" I replied, "Tell me what happened." George then explained how lying in his hospital bed, he had made a long-delayed spiritual decision and immediately sensed a tidal wave of peace sweeping over and through him. He felt changed, renewed, healed.

George's life still ebbs quietly away in these weeks following his mountaintop experience. But he was healed! His body is dying, but his spirit is well. That is a whole other way in which prayer changes things.

GOOD MEDICINE EVEN WHEN GOD SAYS NO

Prayers lift our spirit. Often our body receives the restorative benefits, hastening our health and improving our whole person. Then again, sometimes our soul is healed, and we are renewed, even though our body continues to fail, as it must eventually.

Prayer should be the medicine of choice for everyone, accompanying every conventional remedy and therapy. To omit it is to neglect an acknowledged, effective treatment. Prayer, in a unique and mysterious way, releases God's curative pharmacy of benefits.

Look at the way our Lord prays to our heavenly Father when facing death:

> Then Jesus went with his disciples to a place called Gethsemane, and he said to them, "Sit here while I go over there and pray." . . . and he began to be sorrowful and troubled. Then he said to them, "My soul is overwhelmed with sorrow to the point of death." . . . Going a little farther, he fell with his face to the ground and prayed, "My Father, if it is possible, may this cup be taken from me. Yet not as I will, but as you will."
>
> —MATTHEW 26:36-39

Jesus' prayer in the Garden of Gethsemane blesses us with its passionate simplicity, direct specificity, and mature openheartedness. Overwhelming sorrow grips Jesus. His cry pleads for release from imminent death. No stoic determination defines him—just fear and sorrow. He begs to get out of what he's facing, as anyone

93

HOW DOES JESUS'
PRAYER COMFORT US
AGAINST THE REBUKE
THAT IF WE ONLY
HAD ENOUGH FAITH,
WE'D ALWAYS GET
WHAT WE ASK FOR?

would in such dire straits. Then he turns. "I accept your will, Father," he cries. Jesus models our perfectly appropriate human posture when the unwanted diagnosis or tragic circumstance strikes. He desperately wants to get out of it and goes to the wrestling mat with his Father to try to win a reprieve, a release, a change. But concurrently he shows an accepting attitude. To fight furiously against the threat is always appropriate. To fight with a spirit of acceptance of possible disappointment serves as an antidote to bitterness and most clearly represents mature godliness.

TALKING IT THROUGH

WHY IS IT SO
IMPORTANT FOR US
TO VERBALIZE OUR
FEELINGS? WHAT
DOES THAT DO FOR
US PHYSICALLY,
EMOTIONALLY, AND
SPIRITUALLY?

Prayer is also beneficial because it is conversation with God. Human counselors usually help oppressed people by facilitating the outpouring of thoughts and emotions that they have bottled up inside them. Talking with God helps in the same way. God welcomes honest and open expressions of any and all conflict, confusion, hurt, and anger that we, his children, have stored within us. With perfect understanding and empathy, our heavenly Father hears our prayers and is touched and moved by them. Better than any well-trained therapist, God hears and cares.

We need to talk. Engaging our heavenly Father may be the only truly safe place to get the therapy we need. With God we can set aside all carefulness and speak fully our heart's true feelings. Talking to God frankly and earnestly is a necessary piece in completing the puzzle of our healing.

The Lord is
my shepherd,
I shall not be
in want. . . .
he restores my soul. . . .
Even though I walk
through the valley of
the shadow of death,
I will fear no evil,
for you are with me.

PSALM 23:1, 3, 4

10

OUTLOOKS AND ATTITUDES

*What attitudes and outlooks train children to
grow through adversity?*

The kitty lay dead in the street when we woke up. Shocked and saddened, we prepared a burial spot in the backyard. Gently and reverently we gave thanks for the joy she had brought to our lives, then covered her tiny body. No one spoke of looking for another to take her place. Everyone took the loss seriously and somberly. Then it was over. Our family scattered in a half-dozen directions, onto other things—fun, routine chores, sports, reading—life went on. Grief reentered from time to time, appearing more in one than in another. But no visible interruption marked this loss.

DO WE TEND TO
OVEREMPHASIZE OR
UNDEREMPHASIZE
THE GRIEF THAT
CHILDREN
EXPERIENCE? WHY?

TEACHABLE MOMENTS

When a child is knocked down or bruised by loss or disappointment, the experience presents us with a prime teaching opportunity. But we all too easily miss our chance. For example, we are tempted to quickly brush aside the death of our child's pet as unimportant. Or we may resolve the matter too quickly by getting another pet to replace the one we lost. Neither of these two approaches strengthens our children or instills in them a long-range outlook that stands ready to help them in the future.

HOW CAN WE BE SURE THAT WE ARE TAKING OUR CHILDREN'S PAIN SERIOUSLY ENOUGH WITHOUT "OVERDOING IT"?

Parents and teachers who respect and affirm the distress of their children listen to their feelings. They avoid quick fixes and superficial reassurances. They set a positive table for growth.

Children who are properly equipped to deal with pain discover, without realizing it, that they can face it head-on, survive it, and continue happily on with life. They have not been rescued, sheltered, or belittled. Their pain has been taken with appropriate seriousness—not too much, and not too little. They're treated as being strong enough to handle it.

WHAT KIND OF THEOLOGY OFTEN RESULTS FROM A "GOD TOOK THE KITTY" RESPONSE?

Christian parents may enrich their own empathy by gently assuring their children that the Lord Jesus loves them and therefore hurts for them too in their major childhood loss. However, we need to conscientiously avoid any suggestion that "God took the kitty." That's crucial to the teaching here. Such a fatalistic approach lays the groundwork for some very dangerous theology.

FACE IT

Mature compassion allows discomfort. When we show our children that we are confident that they can face up to their pain, then we're helping them to deal with it. We set the stage for a lifetime of dealing with tough situations head-on, rather than allowing them to deny or avoid them. Fundamental to this approach is the parent's conviction that God has created in humankind, even children, the capacity to heal and grow stronger by facing up to hard times and by going through them.

Christian teaching certainly makes it possible to have this confidence. The most familiar statement supporting Christian hopefulness is Paul's reassurance that "in all things God works for the good" (Rom. 8:28). Although this verse is often misused to deny pain and grief, Paul's words actually undergird the Christian's positive hope and experience. These words should not be sprinkled on open wounds as if they can make them disappear. They should be the ballast in our tanks, the kernel of hope in our hearts, quietly lived out, sturdily leading us forward. We should never use these noble verses to quiet our cries or silence our groans. Rather, they create for us a secure, hopeful environment that frees us when we are bereft to cry fearlessly, confident of a faithful God embracing us.

HOW DIFFERENT WOULD OUR PERSPECTIVE BE IF PAUL HAD WRITTEN "GOD WORKS ALL THINGS FOR THE GOOD" INSTEAD OF "IN ALL THINGS GOD WORKS FOR THE GOOD"?

OPPOSABLE TRAGEDIES

Another potent component of early teaching that prepares children to stalwartly manage tough circumstances is a perspective that sees the harsh events of life as circumstantial, as the result of human error or accident, not as being planned or caused by God. In such a perspective, tragedies are viewed as awful but opposable. We are not seen as helpless victims. We are agents of change, able with God's help to turn every bad thing into something good. With God's help we will find ways to prevent a repetition of life's strong tides of destruction.

The sad, bad, and maddening events of life come from human error, natural disasters, sheer accidents, or a result of sinfulness in people. Christ's Spirit embraces victims and accompanies them through the valley of the shadow of death on into creative reconstruction of their broken lives. God is their partner working for their good, healing, inspiring them to good works, blocking bitterness, instilling hope, negating the spirit of helplessness.

Here lies the clue to why Psalm 23 leads everybody's list of helpful Scriptures. The picture of unfailing companionship and strong support resonates powerfully in the souls of the wounded. Here easy solutions are avoided, and compassionate fellowship is magnified. The deep and difficult valleys and frightening shadows are not denied. But this psalm offers so much hope, comfort, and love. It grants a vision of healing and of arriving out of danger at the other side.

HOW DOES OUR CONFESSION THAT GOD IS ALMIGHTY DIFFER FROM FATALISM, FROM THE IDEA THAT WE ARE POWERLESS BECAUSE EVERYTHING'S "CUT AND DRIED ANYWAY"?

Helpless victimization best describes the mental state of those most unlikely to turn their battered lives back into positive living. The kind of teaching that overemphasizes God's role as sender of trials and temptations easily germinates seeds of helplessness. In contrast, teaching that stresses the companionship, empathy, and compassion of the Lord in the face of life's inevitable breakdowns instills confidence and recovery. Such teaching may even lead us to willingly and intentionally take on suffering as a means of serving God and serving others. We'll take a closer look at that possibility in our last chapter.

The Spirit himself
testifies with our spirit
that we are
God's children.
Now if we are children,
then we are heirs —
heirs of God
and co-heirs with Christ,
if indeed we share
in his sufferings.

> "IF ANYONE WOULD COME AFTER ME, HE MUST DENY HIM-
> SELF AND TAKE UP HIS CROSS AND FOLLOW ME. FOR WHO-
> EVER WANTS TO SAVE HIS LIFE WILL LOSE IT, BUT WHOEVER
> LOSES HIS LIFE FOR ME WILL FIND IT."
>
> *Matthew 16:24-25*

11

INTENTIONAL SUFFERING

*How is suffering for Christ different
than other kinds of suffering?*

The suffering that comes from affliction, the miserable accidents and injuries we sustain from participating in life, is not the same as the suffering we are called to participate in and volunteer for as Christians. We often speak of "having a cross to bear." But impairments, diseases, and losses do not qualify as "crosses." They are afflictions that come to us from various circumstances, through careless-ness or even possibly by genetic predisposition. Suffering for or with Christ is something different.

While they are different, the one kind of suffering may lead to the other. Afflictions may generate spiritual growth in us that may lead us to willingly and intention-ally suffer for Jesus Christ. In fact, suffering for or with Christ may even be exclusively the domain of those who either have been personally knocked down or drawn in

THIS OBSERVATION IS SUPRISING. WHAT DO YOU MAKE OF IT?

closely and empathetically into the pain of others—to the point of feeling and agonizing with them in their help-lessness. Those who know suffering can be turned around by it to willingly take on Christlike suffering as well.

A MATTER OF CHOICE

Suffering for Jesus means to purposely take on an assignment that breaks us out of our comfort zone and introduces us into a state of discomfort. This suffering is voluntary. We can choose not to enter it. Avoiding this type of suffering may be totally acceptable to society. There is no social pressure pushing us to participate in it.

This kind of involvement in suffering with Jesus springs from a divine source. That's because it runs counter to our human nature, which avoids discomfort. That's why suffering for or with Jesus evidences substantial spiritual growth. This kind of living only flows out of suffering when those undergoing it meet God through it.

In the church where I serve we recruit and train scores of volunteers annually to work as counselors on our twenty-four-hour telephone crisis line. One of them, John, I've mentioned earlier. People like John choose to leave their homes once or twice a month for four-hour shifts to answer the calls of the distressed. Willingly entering and feeling the pain of others is a kind of suffering for Christ. We cannot invite others to tell their hurtful story without being impacted emotionally ourselves. So while *suffering* may not be the right word, this activity is akin to it. Although lower on the scale than true suffering, it's a kind of dying for others. It involves deliberately choosing to give up time, energy, and comfort to be compassionately present for someone else.

DOES GOD EXPECT US TO TAKE THIS KIND OF SUFFERING ON OURSELVES? PLEASE EXPLAIN.

This Christian behavior may epitomize spiritual growth. In my experience, those most inclined and best equipped to pursue it are believers who themselves have walked through very difficult valleys.

INVITED TO DIE FOR OTHERS

The life of one of my best friends was saved recently by the courageous efforts of a small group of people. Some were his family members, but two key participants were his colleagues, who acted exclusively out of selfless love and concern. They not only saved his life but also his job and probably his marriage as well. The rescue operation was not a pretty event. But it worked.

Those who managed this dramatic salvage may never be thanked or appreciated for what they did. They walked into the sanctuary of a person caught in the clutches of alcohol addiction and confronted him in every way imaginable. Cornered and pressured, this person's defenses crumbled. He agreed to admit himself to an alcohol treatment center.

Although they saved his life, this man is not at all pleased with them. In fact, he is angry at them. He now despises and rejects all the people who took part. They died for him, and they are continuing to pay a heavy price for doing so.

CAN YOU RELATE SIMILAR EXAMPLES FROM YOUR OWN EXPERIENCE?

There are few examples more dramatic than this one: ordinary folks acting out what Jesus wants, replicating in their own lives something of the dying-for-others that the Lord did for us on the grand scale. People who have been touched by Jesus' sacrifice just *have* to do things like that.

CALLED TO DIVE IN

If there is any theme running through the marching orders Christian people receive from their Lord, it is this: we are called to die for others. We are not instructed to create insulated cells of safety or warm wombs of contentment for ourselves. We are sent out to find times, places, and ways of breaking out of our comfort zones in order to do what's needed.

A number of years ago, my family and I were cruising through the state park at the Ogallala Reservoir in Nebraska, looking for a campsite. Idling along the dirt road we encountered a middle-aged couple running intently toward the water. My thoughts were elsewhere, but my wife said they looked like something was seriously wrong. So I pulled alongside and asked if they needed help. Frantically they pointed toward the reservoir. Without stopping, they cried out, "Our boy is under the water." I braked the car, jumped out, and took off, running in the direction they were headed. I had Linda, four kids, and the dog right on my heels.

When I got to the edge of the water, a young boy was pointing. "He's in there, he's in there, he's in there," he kept crying. I looked around the gathering crowd. The parents hadn't even arrived yet. I thought, "Somebody has to do something." But no one else was moving. In an instant it hit me. *I* had to do it. I quickly stripped down to my underwear and dived in. Nothing. I dived three or four more times. Nothing. Eventually another man joined me in the water. But tiring quickly, I was beginning to fear for my own life. Seconds later we made contact and together brought the youth to shore. Several volunteers tried to resuscitate him. Sadly, we learned the following day that all our efforts had proved futile. The boy had died.

WHAT EXAMPLES CAN YOU GIVE FROM YOUR OWN LIFE OF TIMES WHEN YOU COULD EASILY HAVE DONE NOTHING AND NO ONE WOULD HAVE FAULTED YOU FOR IT, OR EVEN NOTICED? SO *DID* YOU HELP?

Circumstances forced me into action that day. I was compelled by the emergency to dive in, surprised that no one else was doing so. But life is seldom so clear. Usually we can assume or imagine that someone else will do it. Most of the time our inaction is not conspicuous or even noticed at all. Our doing nothing gets lost in the crowd. It's all too easy and ordinary to stand back from what requires risk, time, energy, and potentially even greater forms of self-sacrifice.

A LIFE-ENHANCING KIND OF DYING

The funny thing is that this kind of *dying* to ourselves is actually life-*giving*. Almost always, new, better life flows from actions that break us out of our insulated safety areas—that is, of course, as long as we survive the experience. I nearly drowned at Ogallala Reservoir. If there is no risk, no cost, no discomfort, then it's not really a form of dying.

This is counterculture thinking, the opposite of everyday attitudes that advise us to bypass any challenge that brings us discomfort.

For Jesus, resurrection followed death. That is unique. But there is an intrinsic life principle involved in what Jesus did that extends to us as well: the way to life always goes through death. This is a paradox that radically challenges our instincts. We want to clutch and grasp when we should learn to give up and let loose. In order to save our lives, we must willingly give them up, for if we compulsively hang onto them, we are guaranteed to lose them.

GIVE SOME EXAMPLES WHERE DYING TO OURSELVES CAN BE EASIER TO DO ON THE GRAND SCALE THAN IN THE ROUTINE OF DAILY LIVING.

A young woman consulted me about her dilemma. She was the youngest of three adult children who had recently become parentless. Her mother, the owner of a dress shop, had died, leaving her the store. Her sisters received only small monetary bequests. She didn't feel that was fair. Part of her relished sole ownership. But her Christian convictions prodded her toward equity. Eventually she took legal steps to share everything equally. She died for them, and joy surged in her soul.

This kind of living-through-dying is not demanded of us as if it is the purchase price of our ticket to heaven. That's a gift. But new life always flows from some sort of dying. It grows soul. Dying for others is good for that. But more importantly, it is through that kind of dying that Christ builds God's kingdom. By the Spirit of Jesus, suffering for Christ germinates, nourishes, and guides us into that new life that God gives to all who believe— new life so wondrous that

Never again will they hunger;
    never again will they thirst.
The sun will not beat upon them,
    nor any scorching heat.
For the Lamb at the center of the throne will be their
    shepherd;
    he will lead them to springs of living water.
And God will wipe away every tear from their eyes.
        —REVELATION 7:15-17

POSTSCRIPT

Wise prophets in every age observe that God rarely finds people useful to his purposes who have not been broken by life.

Our suffering, so insidious and pervasive, so unwanted and despised, holds the franchise to unlocking closed hearts and opening barred minds. When the illusion of being in control of our lives shatters, then spiritual empty-handedness begins. That condition spurs us on to spiritual usefulness. Faith begins when spiritual self-sufficiency deflates and proves empty. Usually that takes one kind of smashing or another.

The lovely paradox here is that this is precisely where joy and hope enter. The road to joy always seems to go through sadness and suffering. It's hard to get there any other way. A strong acquaintance with death makes Easter victory brighter. True resurrection joy whispers in the hearts of those stung deeply by lost loved ones. Jesus' embrace means everything to those of us who are truly burdened, legitimately helpless, and weary.

Ironically, spiritual growth involves our personal regression to that childlike dependency Jesus talks about: to become "poor in spirit." Then we are, in Paul's words, "hard pressed on every side, but not crushed; perplexed, but not in despair; persecuted, but not abandoned; struck down, but not destroyed" (2 Cor. 4:8-9).

Healing and renewal come to Jesus' people sooner or later:

Weeping may remain for a night,
> *but rejoicing comes in the morning.*
>> —PSALM 30:5